Thank you for being a Friend

Mfd. for © 2011 DaySpring Cards, Inc., Siloam Springs, AR 72761.

Made in China

D0326152

Human beings who give themselves to relational greatness—
who have friends they laugh with, cry with...
grow old and die with—these are the human beings
who lead magnificent lives.

*JOHN ORTBERG*

Each one of us is God's special work of art.
Through us He teaches and inspires, delights and encourages,
informs and uplifts all those who view our lives.

JONI EARECKSON TADA

We read more deeply, remember more clearly,
enjoy events with greater pleasure
if we have a friend to share with.

PAM BROWN

Let this New Year be the beginning of a new life in each of us wherein "old things are passed away." Let all blessed old things stay, but let the clutter of our heads and hearts be removed, that new inspirations and new affections may come in and gladden our lives.

*CHESTER BURGE EMERSON*

# DECEMBER 28

*Keep on loving one another.... Do not forget to show hospitality to strangers, for by so doing some people have shown hospitality to angels without knowing it.*

HEBREWS 13:1-2 NIV

*Two are better than one, because they have a good reward
for their toil. For if they fall, one will lift up the other.*

ECCLESIASTES 4:9-10 NRSV

Give a friend a phone call or write a letter. Let that person
know he or she is in your thoughts and prayers.
Offer a word of encouragement—the oxygen to the soul.

ALFRED ARMAND MONTAPERT

The gift of friendship among women is a treasure
not to be taken lightly. Women friends become
the face of God to one another—the face of grace,
of delight, of mercy.

*STASI ELDREDGE*

# DECEMBER 26

Behind every joyful Christmas season are busy hands and loving hands that make the memories and then pack it all up for next year, when once again they'll have the joy of unpacking the memories again.

*SANDY LYNAM CLOUGH*

Begin today! No matter how feeble the light,
let it shine as best it may. The world may need
just that quality of light which you have.

*HENRY C. BLINN*

Christmas is the celebration of the keeping of a promise....
A saving promise.

MICHAEL CARD

---

*Suddenly a great company of the heavenly host appeared*
*with the angel, praising God and saying, "Glory to God*
*in the highest heaven, and on earth peace to those*
*on whom His favor rests."*

LUKE 2:13-14 NIV

Encouragement is awesome. It has the capacity to lift
a man's or woman's shoulders.... To breathe fresh fire
into the fading embers of a smoldering dream. To actually
change the course of another human being's day, week, or life.

*CHARLES SWINDOLL*

When God's Son took on flesh, He truly and bodily took on,
out of pure grace, our being, our nature, ourselves.

*DIETRICH BONHOEFFER*

For one human being to love another: that is...
the work for which all other work is but preparation.

*RAINER MARIA RILKE*

# DECEMBER 23

This is and has been the Father's work from the beginning—
to bring us into the home of His heart.

*GEORGE MACDONALD*

---

*Thanks be to God for His indescribable gift!*

2 CORINTHIANS 9:15 NIV

*Dear friends, let us practice loving each other,*
*for love comes from God and those who are loving and kind*
*show that they are the children of God.*

1 JOHN 4:7 TLB

Had my house been filled at Bethlehem,
What should I have done
With that request
Of two for rest?
Would I have guessed
The Prince of Peace was come?

*ALLISON C. WOOD*

God created human beings in His image so they can
be friends—intimate, love-filled companions—
with Him and one another.

*JOHN ORTBERG*

The joy of brightening other lives, bearing each other's burdens, easing others' loads and supplanting empty hearts and lives with generous gifts becomes for us the magic of Christmas.

*W.C. JONES*

Whether we are poets or parents or teachers or artists
or gardeners, we must start where we are and use
what we have. In the process of creation and relationship,
what seems mundane and trivial may show itself
to be a holy, precious, part of a pattern.

*LUCI SHAW*

Love is always bestowed as a gift—freely,
willingly, and without expectation....
We don't love to be loved; we love to love.

Caring and loving must be verbalized if you are going
to be a friend. Your spoken expressions of care
will build a strong bridge.

JIM CONWAY

You don't need candle and fireside glow to make
Christmas happen. Trees, ornaments, gifts, and all of it
are splendid embellishments. Not necessary, but so very nice.
It's Him. He's finding more and more opened inns these days.
It's priceless to discover the pleasure of His company....
May your home know something of all this glory
during these days.

*JACK HAYFORD*

The most beautiful discovery true friends make
is that they can grow separately without growing apart.

*ELISABETH FOLEY*

Friendship is based upon
What we give, not what we take,
And it steers its kindly course
For a special friend's own sake.

*EDITH H. SHANK*

---

*Give generously, for your gifts will return to you later.*

*ECCLESIASTES 11:1 TLB*

*Don't worry about anything; instead, pray about everything;*
*tell God your needs, and don't forget to thank Him for His answers.*

PHILIPPIANS 4:6 TLB

Every day we live is a priceless gift of God,
loaded with possibilities to learn something new,
to gain fresh insights.

*DALE EVANS ROGERS*

Bless every humble soul who, in these days of stress and strain,
preaches sermons without words.

*PETER MARSHALL*

Notice words of compassion. Seek out deeds of kindness.
These are like the doves from heaven, pointing out to you
who are the ones blessed with inner grace and beauty.

CHRISTOPHER DE VINCK

This is the great mystery of Christmas that continues to give us comfort and consolation: we are not alone on our journey. The God of love Who gave us life sent us [the] only Son to be with us at all times and in all places, so that we never have to feel lost in our struggles but always can trust that God walks with us.

*HENRI J. M. NOUWEN*

We never live so intensely as when we love strongly.
We never realize ourselves so vividly as when we are
in the full glow of love for others.

WALTER RAUSCHENBUSCH

*Be completely humble and gentle; be patient,*
*bearing with one another in love.*

EPHESIANS 4:2 NIV

*When others are happy, be happy with them.*
*If they are sad, share their sorrow.*

ROMANS 12:15 TLB

God's birth in a barn has made a statement to the world
ever since: it doesn't matter where you're born
or the condition of your surroundings; you can accomplish
His ordained purpose for your life.

*THELMA WELLS*

One of the most important responsibilities
in the Christian life is to care about others,
smile at them, and be a friend to the friendless.

*JAMES DOBSON*

The joy of receiving is in far more than the gifts—that when we receive graciously and gladly, we reciprocate the gift with joy and gratitude; and in that moment of shared happiness and understanding, giver and receiver "connect."

*JENNY WALTON*

A keen sense of humor helps us to overlook the unbecoming,
understand the unconventional, tolerate the unpleasant,
overcome the unexpected, and outlast the unbearable.

*BILLY GRAHAM*

# DECEMBER 10

I know now that the world is not filled with strangers.
It is full of other people—waiting only to be spoken to.

*BETH DAY*

We encounter God in the ordinariness of life,
not in the search for spiritual highs and extraordinary,
mystical experiences but in our simple presence in life.

BRENNAN MANNING

# DECEMBER 9

The person who tries to live alone will not succeed
as a human being. His heart withers if it does not answer
another heart. His mind shrinks away if he hears only the echoes
of his own thoughts and finds no other inspiration.

*PEARL BUCK*

I have never been a millionaire. But I have enjoyed
a crackling fire, a glorious sunset, a walk with a friend....
There are plenty of life's tiny delights for all of us.

JACK ANTHONY

Caring words, friendship, affectionate touch—all of these have a healing quality. Why? Because we were all created by God to give and receive love.

*JACK FROST*

Peace is when time doesn't matter as it passes by.

*MARIA SCHNELL*

---

*Live in peace with each other.*

*ROMANS* 12:16 NCV

*In response to all He has done for us, let us outdo each other*
*in being helpful and kind to each other and in doing good.*

*HEBREWS 10:24 TLB*

The one who loves with God's love will not flatter,
or hide anything from his friend, no matter how difficult
it may be to say…. You should be very happy
if you are given a friend who loves you in this way—
that is, a friend who wants to see you progress in spirit
and become more like Christ.

*TERESA of AVILA (Paraphrased by David Hazard)*

A friend doesn't go on a diet because you are fat.
A friend never defends a husband who gets his wife
an electric skillet for her birthday. A friend will tell you
she saw your old boyfriend—and he's a priest.

*ERMA BOMBECK*

Kind words smooth all the paths of life
And smiles make burdens light,
And uncomplaining friends can make
A daytime out of night.

*CARRIE JACOBS BOND*

If God had a refrigerator, your picture would be put on it....
He sends you flowers every spring and a sunrise
every morning.... Face it, friend. He's crazy about you.

*MAX LUCADO*

Whoever walks toward God one step,
God runs toward him two.

*JEWISH PROVERB*

---

*Let us come boldly to the very throne of God.*

*HEBREWS 4:16 TLB*

If the friend is close at hand, that is best; but if he is far away,
he still is there to think of, to wonder about, to hear from,
to write to, to share life and experience with, to serve,
to honor, to admire, to love.

*ARTHUR CHRISTOPHER BENSON*

Who but a good friend would put her life on hold
in order to listen, advise, sympathize, and send you
on your way secure in the knowledge that someone cares?

*LOIS WYSE*

*I am leaving you with a gift—peace of mind and heart!*
*And the peace I give isn't fragile like the peace the world gives.*
*So don't be troubled or afraid. Remember what I told you—*
*I am going away, but I will come back to you again.*

JOHN 14:27-28 TLB

*And when we obey Him, every path He guides us
on is fragrant with His loving kindness and His truth.*

PSALM 25:10 TLB

The goal of grace is to create a love relationship
between God and us who believe, the kind of relationship
for which we were first made.

*J.I. PACKER*

What we lack is not so much leisure to do as time to reflect and time to feel. What we seldom "take" is time to experience the things that have happened, the things that are happening, the things that are still ahead of us.

*MARGARET MEAD and RHODA METRAUX*

Half the joy of life is in little things taken on the run.
Let us run if we must...but let us keep our hearts young
and our eyes open that nothing worth our while
shall escape us. And everything is worth its while
if we only grasp it and its significance.

*VICTOR CHERBULIEZ*

Friends are angels who lift our feet when our own wings
have trouble remembering how to fly.

Though weary, love is not tired;
Though pressed, it is not straitened;
Though alarmed, it is not confounded
Love securely passes through all.

*THOMAS À KEMPIS*

Time alone with God can help us grow,
but so can serving others. Instead of feeling guilty
about how little time alone I get, I need to look at how
I can connect with God in the midst of my chaos.

*KERI WYATT KENT*

No man is an iceberg drifting on the ocean of history.
Each one of us belongs to a great family, in which he has
his own place and his own role to play.

*POPE JOHN PAUL II*

Contentment comes as the infallible result of great acceptances,
great humilities — of not trying to make ourselves
this or that, but of surrendering ourselves to the fullness
of life — of letting life flow through us.

*DAVID GRAYSON*

*Whenever we pray for you, we always begin by giving thanks to God the Father of our Lord Jesus Christ.*

COLOSSIANS 1:3 TLB

*Don't worry about whether you have enough food to eat
or clothes to wear. For life consists of far more than food
and clothes. Look at the ravens—they don't plant or harvest
or have barns to store away their food, and yet they
get along all right—for God feeds them. And you are
far more valuable to Him than any birds!*

LUKE 12:22-24 TLB

As white snowflakes fall quietly and thickly on a winter day,
answers to prayer will settle down upon you
at every step you take.... The story of your life
will be the story of prayer and answers to prayer.

OLE HALLESBY

When you come to the edge of all the light you have
and must take a step into the darkness of the unknown,
believe that one of two things will happen.
Either there will be something solid for you
to stand on — or you will be taught how to fly.

*PATRICK OVERTON*

Hands down, Thanksgiving is my favorite holiday.
It highlights the home and family. It is synonymous
with stuff that can be found only at home—
early morning fussing around in the kitchen,
kids and grandkids, long distance phone calls,
holding hands and praying before that special meal.

CHARLES SWINDOLL

Friendship is usually treated by the majority of mankind
as a tough and everlasting thing which will survive
all manner of bad treatment. But...it should be dealt with
delicately and tenderly being as it is a sensitive plant
and not a roadside thistle.

*OUIDA*

My friends have made the story of my life.
In a thousand ways they have turned my limitations
into beautiful privileges, and enabled me to walk
serene and happy in the shadow cast by my deprivation.

*HELEN KELLER*

Life is not intended to be simply a round of work,
no matter how interesting and important that work may be.
A moment's pause to watch the glory of a sunrise
or a sunset is soul satisfying, while a bird's song
will set the steps to music all day long.

*LAURA INGALLS WILDER*

Madam, I have been looking for a person who disliked gravy all my life; let us swear eternal friendship.

*SYDNEY SMITH*

If there has come to us the miracle of friendship,
if there is a soul to which our soul has been drawn,
it is surely worthwhile being loyal and true.

*HUGH BLACK*

Thanksgiving puts power in living, because it opens
the generators of the heart to respond gratefully,
to receive joyfully, and to react creatively.

When you are in the dark, listen,
and God will give you a very precious message
for someone else when you get into the light.

*OSWALD CHAMBERS*

---

*God has comforted us—and this, too, to help you; to show you*
*from our personal experience how God will tenderly comfort you*
*when you undergo these same sufferings.*

2 CORINTHIANS 1:6-7 TLB

The opportunity that God sends
does not wake up one who is asleep.

*SENEGALESE PROVERB*

---

*Now choose life, so that you and your children may live
and that you may love the Lord your God, listen to His voice,
and hold fast to Him.*

*DEUTERONOMY 30:19-20 NIV*

Silences make the real conversations between friends.
Not the saying but the never needing to say is what counts.

*MARGARET LEE RUNBECK*

A true friend is the greatest of all blessings,
and the one which we take least thought to acquire.

*FRANCOIS DUC DE LA ROCHEFOUCAULD*

Reflection...enables our minds to be stretched
in three different directions—the direction that leads
to a proper relationship with God, the relationship that leads
to a healthy relationship with others, and the relationship
that leads to a deeper understanding of oneself.

MARK CONNOLLY

With God there is always more unfolding,
that what we can glimpse of the divine is always
exactly enough, and never enough.

*KATHLEEN NORRIS*

A friend is one who joyfully sings with you
when you are on the mountain top,
and silently beside you through the valley.

*WILLIAM A. WARD*

Live today fully, expressing gratitude for all you have been,
all you are right now, and all you are becoming.

*MELODIE BEATTIE*

God came to us because God wanted to join us on the road,
to listen to our story, and help us realize that we are not walking
in circles but moving toward the house of peace and joy.

*HENRI M. NOUWEN*

*O Lord, what a variety You have made! And in wisdom
You have made them all! The earth is full of Your riches.*

PSALM 104:24 TLB

The ability to simplify means to eliminate the unnecessary
so that the necessary may speak.

HANS HOFMANN

---

*The only thing that counts is faith expressing itself through love.*

GALATIANS 5:6 NIV

The capacity for caring illuminates any relationship.
The more people you care about, the more intensely you care,
the more alive you are.

You can make more friends in two months
by becoming interested in other people than you can
in two years by trying to get other people interested in you.

*DALE CARNEGIE*

The best friendships have weathered misunderstandings
and trying times. One of the secrets of a good relationship
is the ability to accept the storms.

*ALAN LOY MCGINNIS*

True love possesses the ability to see beyond....
It sees beneath the veneer. Love focuses on the soul.
Love sees another's soul in great need of help
and sets compassion to work.

*CHARLES SWINDOLL*

Gratitude…takes nothing for granted,
is never unresponsive, is constantly awakening
to new wonder and to praise of the goodness of God.

*THOMAS MERTON*

Kindness is given so softly, so gently, falling like tiny seeds along our paths — and brightening them with flowers.

PAM BROWN

Look deep within yourself and recognize what brings life
and grace into your heart. It is this that can be shared
with those around you. You are loved by God.
This is an inspiration to love.

*CHRISTOPHER DE VINCK*

There never was any heart truly great and generous,
that was not also tender and compassionate.

*ROBERT SOUTH*

*O give thanks to the Lord, for He is good;*
*for His steadfast love endures forever.*

PSALM 107:1 NRSV

# FEBRUARY 17

*If you love someone, you will be loyal to him no matter what the cost.*
*You will always believe in him, always expect the best of him,*
*and always stand your ground in defending him.*

1 CORINTHIANS 13:7 TLB

Tuck [this] thought into your heart today.
Treasure it. Your Father God cares about
your daily everythings that concern you.

*KAY ARTHUR*

Walk and talk and work and laugh with your friends,
but behind the scenes, keep up with the life
of simple prayer and inward worship.

*THOMAS R. KELLY*

Friendship is like love at its best: not blind but sympathetically
all-seeing; a support which does not wait for understanding;
an act of faith which does not need, but always has, reason.

LOUIS UNTERMEYER

Love is extravagant in the price it is willing to pay,
the time it is willing to give, the hardships it is willing
to endure, and the strength it is willing to spend.
Love never thinks in terms of "how little",
but always in terms of "how much." Love gives,
love knows, and love lasts.

JONI EARECKSON TADA

Every time you smile at someone, it is an action of love,
a gift to that person, a beautiful thing.

*MOTHER TERESA*

Indeed, we do not really live unless we have friends
surrounding us like a firm wall
against the winds of the world.

*CHARLES HANSON TOWNE*

If we learn how to give ourselves, to forgive others,
and to live with thanksgiving, we need not seek happiness.
It will seek us.

Everything in life is most fundamentally a gift.
And you receive it best, and you live it best,
by holding it with very open hands.

*LEO O'DONOVAN*

*He surrounds me with loving-kindness and tender mercies.*
*He fills my life with good things!*

PSALM 103:4-5 TLB

People need to be encouraged. Here's the challenge:
send an e-mail this week that the recipient will not delete.
Send a note in the mail that will be saved for years. Leave an
encouraging voice mail that will be saved for a long time.
Go up to someone and just do whatever you can
to encourage as an expression of Christian love.

*LEITH ANDERSON*

Helping and serving in friendship
seals our need for each other and gives us a sense
of personal fulfillment and satisfaction.

*JERRY AND MARY WHITE*

We are God's idea. We are His.... Look deeply into the face of every human being on earth, and you will see His likeness.

*MAX LUCADO*

Good communication is stimulating as black coffee,
and just as hard to sleep after.

ANNE MORROW LINDBERGH

There are no little things. "Little things," so called
are the hinges of the universe.

*FANNY FERN*

---

*Let us try to do what makes peace and helps one another.*

*ROMANS 14:19 NCV*

Grace and gratitude belong together like heaven and earth.
Grace evokes gratitude like the voice an echo.
Gratitude follows grace as thunder follows lightning.

*KARL BARTH*

C.S. Lewis once surmised that each person is created to see a different facet of God's beauty—something no one else can see in quite the same way—and then to bless all worshipers through all eternity with an aspect of God they could not otherwise see.

*JOHN ORTBERG*

Words cannot express the joy which a friend imparts;
they only can know who have experienced. A friend is dearer
than the light of heaven, for it would be better
for us that the sun were extinguished than that
we should be without friends.

JOHN CHRYSOSTOM

Heaven comes down to touch us when we find ourselves
safe in the heart of another.

*Those who hope in the Lord will renew their strength.*
*They will soar on wings like eagles; they will run*
*and not grow weary, they will walk and not be faint.*

ISAIAH 40:31 NIV

*Encourage one another and build each other up,
just as in fact you are doing.*

1 THESSALONIANS 5:11 NIV

Something deep in all of us yearns for God's beauty,
and we can find it no matter where we are.

SUE MONK KIDD

There is not enough darkness in all the world to put out the light of one small candle...any reminder of something deeply felt or dearly loved. No [one] is as poor as not to have many of these small candles. When they are lighted, darkness goes away and a touch of wonder remains.

ARTHUR GORDON

When I look back upon my early days I am stirred
by the thought of the number of people whom I have to thank
for what they gave me or for what they were to me.

*ALBERT SCHWEITZER*

Friendships begun in this world can be taken up again
in heaven, never to be broken off.

*FRANCIS DE SALES*

God has given us two hands—one to receive with
and the other to give with. We are not cisterns
made for hoarding. We are channels made for sharing.

*BILLY GRAHAM*

The place where two friends first met is sacred to them
all through their friendship, all the more sacred
as their friendship deepens and grows old.

*PHILLIPS BROOKS*

Heavenly Father, teach me not to procrastinate
but to do what I can today, because there is no promise
of tomorrow. Lead me to those people who are in need
of something that I can give. I want to be available for You
to use in any way that You should choose. Amen.

*KIM BOYCE*

God's heart is the most sensitive and tender of all.
No act goes unnoticed, no matter how insignificant or small.

*RICHARD J. FOSTER*

*The Lord is always good. He is always loving and kind,*
*and His faithfulness goes on and on to each succeeding generation.*

PSALM 100:5 TLB

*Let Him have all your worries and cares,*
*for He is always thinking about you*
*and watching everything that concerns you.*

1 PETER 5:7 TLB

Love to me is when you walk out on that "one more thing" and say, "Nothing will come between you and me. Not even one thing."

*SARA GROVES*

Blessed are they who tenderly seek to comfort another
and never run out of compassion and grace.

*JANET L. WEAVER SMITH*

The wonder of living is held within the beauty of silence,
the glory of sunlight, the sweetness of fresh spring air,
the quiet strength of earth, and the love that lies
at the very root of all things.

To be glad of life, because it gives you the chance to love
and to work and to play and to look up at the stars;…
to think seldom of your enemies, often of your friends,
and every day of Christ; and to spend as much time as you can,
with body and with spirit in God's out-of-doors—
these are little guideposts on the footpath to peace.

*HENRY VAN DYKE*

God says to His children:
Are you lonesome? Breathe out My name.
Come to Me and I will be your friend.
Are you sick? Come to Me for healing.
Are you left out of things? Feeling rejected
and pushed aside? Come home to Me.

*ALICE CHAPIN*

When God gives a friend, He is entrusting us with the care
of another's heart. It is a chance to…be a Life giver.

*STASI ELDREDGE*

Biblical love is "action in the best interest of the other person." Ultimately it would be good to feel love *and* do love, but loving others is most about the doing. In other words, Christians love others even when we don't feel like it. Love is what we *do.*

LEITH ANDERSON

We may not be the kind of people we want to be,
we may be a long way from our goals, we may have
more failures than achievements, we may not be wealthy
or powerful or spiritual, we may not even be happy,
but we are nonetheless accepted by God, held in His Hands.

*MCCULLOUGH*

*Let us not become weary in doing good, for at the proper time
we will reap a harvest if we do not give up. Therefore, as we
have opportunity, let us do good to all people.*

GALATIANS 6:9-10 NIV

*The steadfast love of the Lord never ceases,*
*His mercies never come to an end;*
*they are new every morning;*
*great is Your faithfulness.*

LAMENTATIONS 3:22-23 NRSV

God has a wonderful plan for each person....
He knew even before He created this world
what beauty He would bring forth from our lives.

*LOUIS B. WYLY*

There is in friendship something of all relations,
and something above them all. It is the golden thread
that ties the hearts of all the world.

*JOHN EVELYN*

You have an instrument and a song, and you owe it to God
to play them both sublimely.

*MAX LUCADO*

---

*Thank you for making me so wonderfully complex!*
*It is amazing to think about. Your workmanship is marvelous.*

*PSALM 139:14 TLB*

When you're with someone you trust in,
never needing to pretend,
Someone who helps you know yourself...
you know you're with a friend.

*AMANDA BRADLEY*

Meeting someone for the first time
is like going on a treasure hunt.
What wonderful worlds
we can find in others!

*EDWARD E. FORD*

Love is the true means by which the world is enjoyed:
our love to others, and others' love to us.

*THOMAS TRAHERNE*

Dust if you must, but there's not much time,
with rivers to swim and mountains to climb, music to hear
and books to read, friends to cherish and life to lead.

A good friend is a connection to life —
a tie to the past, a road to the future.

*LOIS WYSE*

What the dew is to the flower, gentle words are to the soul.
*POLLY RUPE*

---

*Your gentleness has made me great.*

*PSALM 18:35 TLB*

*Be beautiful inside, in your hearts, with the lasting charm*
*of a gentle and quiet spirit that is so precious to God.*

1 PETER 3:4 TLB

No one can develop freely in this world and find a full life without feeling understood by at least one person.

*PAUL TOURNIER*

We must love our friends as true amateurs love paintings;
they have their eyes perpetually fixed on the fine parts,
and see no others.

*MADAM D'EPINAY*

O hushed October morning mild,
Begin the hours of this day slow.
Make the day seem to us less brief.
Hearts not averse to being beguiled.

*ROBERT FROST*

If you surrender completely to the moments as they pass,
you live more richly those moments.

ANNE MORROW LINDBERGH

A friend understands what you are trying to say,
even when our thoughts aren't fitting into words.

*ANN D. PARRISH*

Life is short and we never have enough time for gladdening
the hearts of those who travel the way with us.
O, be swift to love! Make haste to be kind.

*HENRI FRÉDÉRIC AMIEL*

Don't think that the details of your day are too insignificant to bring before God. If He cares enough about the hairs on your head to number them, then surely He cares about the things that fill your day.

*STORMIE OMARTIAN*

Reach high, for stars lie hidden in your soul.
Dream deep, for every dream precedes the goal.

PAMELA VAULL STARR

*God's peace...is far more wonderful than the human mind
can understand. His peace will keep your thoughts and your hearts
quiet and at rest as you trust in Christ Jesus.*

PHILIPPIANS 4:7 TLB

*Dear friends, now we are children of God, and what we will be has not yet been made known. But we know that when Christ appears, we shall be like Him, for we shall see Him as He is.*

1 JOHN 3:2 NIV

Night jasmine blooming brings memories flooding through
my mind of a screened-in porch at twilight, the quiet hum
of a ceiling fan, the squeak of a white-wicker rocker,
an icy glass of lemonade, intimate conversation
with a treasured friend, and time...time just to be.

A happy life is...built up of...little clumps of violets
noticed by the roadside, hidden away almost so
that only those can see them who have
God's peace and love in their hearts.

*EDWARD WILSON*

God loves to look at us, and loves it when we will look back at Him. Even when we try to run away from our troubles… God will find us, bless us, even when we feel most alone, unsure…. God will find a way to let us know that He is with us *in this place*, wherever we are.

*KATHLEEN NORRIS*

Choose your friend wisely,
Test your friend well;
True friends, like rarest gems,
Prove hard to tell.
Winter him, summer him.
Know your friend well.

The real art of conversation is not only to say
the right thing in the right place but to leave unsaid
the wrong thing at the tempting moment.

*DOROTHY NEVILL*

Only He who created the wonders of the world
entwines hearts in an eternal way.

May you always find three welcomes in life,

In a garden during summer,

At a fireside during winter,

And whatever the day or season,

In the kind eyes of a friend.

You were prescribed and then presented to this world
exactly as God arranged it.

*CHARLES SWINDOLL*

---

*God's ways are as mysterious as...the manner in which
a human spirit is infused into the little body of a baby
while it is yet in its mother's womb.*

*ECCLESIASTES 11:5 TLB*

*He knows the number of hairs on your head!*
*Never fear, you are far more valuable to Him*
*than a whole flock of sparrows.*

LUKE 12:7 TLB

People who deal with life generously and large-heartedly
go on multiplying relationships to the end.

ARTHUR CHRISTOPHER BENSON

Good humor is a tonic for mind and body.
It is the best antidote for anxiety and depression.
It is a business asset. It attracts and keeps friends.
It lightens human burdens. It is the direct route
to serenity and contentment.

*GRENVILLE KLEISER*

I cannot count the number of times I have been strengthened
by another's heartfelt hug, appreciative note, surprise gift,
or caring questions.... My friends are an oasis to me,
encouraging me to go on. They are essential to my well-being.

*DEE BRESTIN*

Don't let artificial light and city streets keep you
from noticing sunsets and sunrises, from experiencing
the spring of new life and the harvest of fall.

M. BASIL PENNINGTON

Every day at work, home, school, and play, God presents us with opportunities to be a blessing to people who may not be as nice to us as we deserve or desire. In the middle of these opportunities He strengthens us and enables us to pay back good for evil.

*THELMA WELLS*

Life is fortified by many friendships. To love, and to be loved,
is the greatest happiness of existence.

*SYDNEY SMITH*

Many people will walk in and out of your life;
only true friends will leave footprints in your heart.

Every time you forgive someone who hurt you,
encourage someone who feels defeated, extend compassion
to someone who stands alone, confront someone in love,
open your heart to a friend, reconcile with an enemy,
devote time to a child, you align yourself
with God's central purpose in this world.

*JOHN ORTBERG*

A true friend is someone who listens to us
with real concentration and expresses sincere care
for our struggles and pains. She makes us feel
that something very deep is happening to us.

*SISTER HELEN FEENEY*

*No eye has seen, nor ear heard, nor the human heart conceived,
what God has prepared for those who love Him.*

1 CORINTHIANS 2:9 NRSV

*Above all, clothe yourselves with love,*
*which binds everything together in perfect harmony.*

COLOSSIANS 3:14 NRSV

I'd like to be the sort of friend that you have been to me,
I'd like be the help that you've been always glad to be;
I'd like to mean as much to you each minute of the day.
As you have meant, old friend of mine, to me along the way.

*EDGAR A. GUEST*

We must ruthlessly eliminate hurry from our lives.

Hurry is not just a disordered schedule.

Hurry is a disordered heart.

*JOHN ORTBERG*

My neighbor is not the person who is like me, whose skin
is the same color, whose bank account is roughly equal to mine.
They need not be from the same culture or country.
All that makes a person my neighbor, says Jesus [in the parable
of the Good Samaritan], is their need of my mercy.

MICHAEL CARD

Enjoy the little things. One day you will look back
and realize that those little things
were the most important things of all.

The tiniest dewdrop hanging from a grass blade
in the morning is big enough to reflect the sunshine
and the blue of the sky.

It's the little things we do and say
that mean so much as we go our way.
A kindly deed can lift a load
from weary shoulders on the road.

*WILLA HOEY*

The true spirit of conversation consists in building on another man's observation, not overturning it.

*EDWARD G. BULWER-LYTTON*

The purpose of life, after all, is to live it, to taste experience
to the utmost, to reach out eagerly without fear
for newer and richer experiences.

*ELEANOR ROOSEVELT*

*May...Christ Himself and God our Father,*
*who loved us and by His grace gave us eternal encouragement*
*and good hope, encourage your hearts and strengthen you*
*in every good deed and word.*

2 THESSALONIANS 2:16-17 NIV

*My prayer for you is that you will overflow more and more with love for others, and at the same time keep on growing in spiritual knowledge and insight.*

PHILIPPIANS 1:9 TLB

The secret of life is that all we have and are
is a gift of grace to be shared.

LLOYD JOHN OGILVIE

Heavenly Father, Thank You for the opportunity to laugh.
Help me to find joy in everything that I do. Let me laugh
and be cheerful, so that those around me will be blessed
by my smile and my optimism. Amen.

*KIM BOYCE*

Friends are of utmost importance. We love, trust, get hurt, sometimes get mad, but we love and trust anyhow, because that's the best way to let our friendship grow.

The first blush of friendship is a grace to behold:
a moment of shyness, a tentative hello. Every other gift in life
takes wing from here—affection, generosity, sharing—
until soon your life is rich.

Jesus was a gentle person. Wherever true Christianity
has gone, His followers have performed
acts of gentleness and kindness.

*BILLY GRAHAM*

Once the realization is accepted that even between
the closest human beings infinite distances continue to exist,
a wonderful living side by side can grow up, if they succeed
in loving the distance between them which makes it possible
for each to see the other whole against the sky.

*RAINER MARIA RILKE*

Think of someone who recently offended, hurt, neglected, angered or otherwise antagonized you and decide to let it go. Just release any resentment and move on.

*LEITH ANDERSON*

We are all travelers in…the wilderness of this world,
and the best that we find in our travels is an honest friend.
She is a fortunate voyager who finds many. We travel indeed
to find them. They are the end and the reward of life.
They keep us worthy of ourselves, and when we are alone,
we are only nearer to the absent.

*ROBERT LOUIS STEVENSON*

*Bear with each other and forgive one another*
*if any of you has a grievance against someone.*
*Forgive as the Lord forgave you.*

COLOSSIANS 3:13 NIV

*May God bless you richly and grant you increasing freedom from all anxiety and fear.*

1 PETER 1:2 TLB

I thank God far more for friends than for my daily bread—
for friendship is the bread of the heart.

MARY MITFORD

How far you go in life depends on your being tender with the young, compassionate with the aged, sympathetic with the striving, and tolerant of the weak and the strong— because someday in life you will be all of these.

GEORGE WASHINGTON CARVER

First it is necessary to stand on your own two feet.
But the minute you find yourself in that position,
the next thing you should do is reach out
your arms for a friend.

*KRISTIN HUNTER LATTANY*

If a man does not make new acquaintances,
as he advances through life, he will soon
find himself left alone. A man...should keep
his friendship in constant repair.

*SAMUEL JOHNSON*

The more the pleasures of the body fade away,
the greater to me is the pleasure and charm of conversation.

*PLATO*

I wish you sunshine on your path and storms
to season your journey. I wish you peace—in the world
in which you live and in the smallest corner of the heart
where truth is kept. I wish you faith—to help define
your living and your life. More I cannot wish you—
except perhaps love—to make all the rest worthwhile.

ROBERT A. WARD

If a friend loves me, I'm not left wondering about the status of our relationship; she'll tell me. If a friend truly loves me, I won't wonder if my words were too direct or my behavior troubling; she'll tell me. There is nothing like the truth.

MARILYN MEBERG

Dare to love and to be a real friend. The love you give
and receive is a reality that will lead you closer and closer
to God as well as those whom God has given you to love.

*HENRI J.M. NOUWEN*

*These are the things that you shall do:*
*Speak the truth to one another, render...judgments*
*that are true and make for peace.*

ZECHARIAH 8:16 NRSV

Jesus wants to be our friend. He doesn't want us to walk alone. But it's not just that He wants us to be with Him; it's that He wants to be with us!

*LEITH ANDERSON*

---

*Greater love has no one than this: to lay down one's life for one's friends. You are My friends if you do what I command.*

*JOHN 15:13-14 NIV*

When I recollect the treasure of friendship that has been bestowed upon me, I withdraw all charges against life. If much has been denied me, much, very much, has been given me. So long as the memory of certain beloved friends lives in my heart, I shall say that life is good.

*HELEN KELLER*

I expect to pass through life but once. If, therefore,
there can be any kindness I can show, or any good thing
I can do to any fellow being, let me do it now...
as I shall not pass this way again.

WILLIAM PENN

Each of us may be sure that if God sends us on stony paths
He will provide us with strong shoes, and He will not send us
out on any journey for which He does not equip us well.

*ALEXANDER MACLAREN*

We have been in God's thought from all eternity,
and in His creative love, His attention never leaves us.

*MICHAEL QUOIST*

My friends have always been hope bearers for me
by reflecting Christ's love both in my early years of struggle
and today. [They] have been like zany mirrors for me
in that they assure me that my cockeyed reflection
is both accurate and acceptable.

*PATSY CLAIRMONT*

Grant me still a friend

In my retreat,

Whom I may whisper,

Solitude is sweet.

WILLIAM COWPER

The great acts of love are done by those
who are habitually performing small acts of kindness.

Love is always free to love, and arms are always stretched as wide as the cross toward anyone who needs to be loved.

*EUGENIA PRICE*

"For the mountains may depart and the hills disappear,
but My kindness shall not leave you. My promise of peace for you
will never be broken," says the Lord who has mercy upon you.

ISAIAH 54:10 TLB

*If you love those who love you, what reward will you get?...*
*And if you greet only your own people, what are you doing*
*more than others?... Be perfect, therefore,*
*as your heavenly Father is perfect.*

MATTHEW 5:46-48 NIV

Life begins each morning…. Each morning is the open door
to a new world—new vistas, new aims, new tryings.

*LEIGH HODGES*

A person who is given words of beauty
is a person who will express beauty....
All beauty can be traced, ultimately, to God.

*CHRISTOPHER DE VINCK*

Line by line, moment by moment, special times
are etched into our memories in the permanent ink
of everlasting love in our relationships.

*GLORIA GAITHER*

Love builds memories that endure, to be treasured up
as hints of what shall be hereafter.

*BEDE JARRET*

The heart hath its own memory, like the mind,
And in it are enshrined
The precious keepsakes, into which is wrought
The giver's loving thought.

*LONGFELLOW*

Friendships need to be nurtured and guarded and fought for.
We need to call one another without waiting to be called first.
We need to ask how our friends are doing and really listen
to their answers. Listen between the lines.

*STASI ELDREDGE*

When you set out on a journey and night covers the road,

you don't conclude that the road has vanished.

And how else could we discover the stars?

The human heart, at whatever age,
opens to the heart that opens in return.

MARIA EDGEWORTH

They say you will never be lonely from the start of each day to its end if you walk life's pathway with love in your heart and side by side with a friend.

*A friend loves at all times.*

PROVERBS 17:17 NIV

*I have loved you with an everlasting love;*
*therefore I have continued My faithfulness to you.*

JEREMIAH 31:3 NRSV

There is joy in heaven when a tear of sorrow is shed
in the presence of a truly understanding heart.
And heaven will never forget that joy.

*CHARLES MALIK*

The very possibility of friendship with God transfigures life.
This conviction...tends inevitably to deepen
every human friendship, to make it vastly more significant.

HENRY CHURCHILL KING

Two roads diverged in a wood, and I—
I took the one less traveled by,
And that has made all the difference.

*ROBERT FROST*

I count your friendship one of the chiefest pleasures
of my life, a comfort in time of doubt and trouble,
a joy in time of prosperity and success,
and an inspiration at all times.

EDWIN OSGOOD GROVER

Intimacy may not be rushed.... Inwardness is time-consuming,
open only to minds willing to sample spirituality
in small bites, savoring each one.

*CALVIN MILLER*

When we take time to notice the simple things in life,
we never lack for encouragement. We discover
we are surrounded by a limitless hope
that's just wearing everyday clothes.

Dear friends, no matter how we find them, are as essential
to our lives as breathing in and breathing out.

*LOIS WYSE*

Being with you is like walking on a very clear morning—
definitely the sensation of belonging there.

*E.B.WHITE*

Nothing enters your life accidentally—remember that.
Behind our every experience is our loving, sovereign God.

CHARLES SWINDOLL

---

*You both precede and follow me and place Your hand of blessing*
*on my head.*

PSALM 139:5 TLB

*You saw me before I was born and scheduled each day of my life before I began to breathe. Every day was recorded in Your book! How precious it is, Lord, to realize that You are thinking about me constantly!*

PSALM 139:16-17 TLB

We must drink deeply from the very Source, the deep calm
and peace of interior quietude and refreshment of God,
allowing the pure water of divine grace to flow plentifully
and unceasingly from the Source itself.

*MOTHER TERESA*

To have someone who wants to absorb us, who wants
to understand the shape and structure of our lives,
who will listen for more than our words,
is one of friendship's greatest gifts.

*PAUL D. ROBBINS*

It is loving, and not by being loved,
that one can come nearest the soul of another.

*GEORGE MACDONALD*

Love is not about what we do, but who we are,
convincing others of our love for them…
and about who loves us.

*JACK FROST*

Compassion means to lay a bridge over to the other without knowing whether he wants to be reached.

*HENRI J.M. NOUWEN*

Little acts of kindness which we render to each other
in everyday life are like flowers by the wayside
to the traveler: they serve to gladden the heart
and relieve the tedium of life's journey.

*EUNICE BATHRICK*

Friendship is not diminished by distance or time...
by suffering or silence. It is in these things that it roots
most deeply. It is from these things that it flowers.

PAM BROWN

Your greatest pleasure is that which rebounds
from hearts that you have made glad.

*HENRY WARD BEECHER*

*You should be like one big happy family, full of sympathy toward each other, loving one another with tender hearts and humble minds.*

1 PETER 3:8 TLB

*The Lord your God is with you....*
*He will take great delight in you;*
*in His love He will...rejoice over you with singing.*

ZEPHANIAH 3:17 NIV

Now may the warming love of friends
Surround you as you go
Down the path of light and laughter
Where the happy memories grow.

*HELEN LOWRIE MARSHALL*

God's love is unreasonable. After all, He gave
what He loved most, His Son, for those who cared not at all.
Can you imagine that kind of immense, intense love?

*PATSY CLAIRMONT*

Who we are is connected to those we love
and to those who have influenced us toward goodness.

*CHRISTOPHER DE VINCK*

Time is a very precious gift from God—so precious
that it's only given to us moment by moment.

*AMELIA BARR*

God's love never ceases. Never.... Our faith does not
earn it any more than our stupidity jeopardizes it.
God doesn't love us less if we fail or more if we succeed.
God's love never ceases.

*MAX LUCADO*

We sat on the edge of the earth, with our feet dangling over the side, and marveled that we had found each other.

*ERIK DILLARD*

It is ironic that we try to impress people by saying clever
or funny things, yet nothing binds one human being
to another more than the sense that they have been deeply,
carefully listened to. It is no accident that we speak
of paying attention to people; attention is
the most valuable currency we have.

*JOHN ORTBERG*

There's something beautiful about finding
one's innermost thoughts in another.

*OLIVER SCHREINER*

Talking comes by nature, silence by wisdom.

*AMERICAN PROVERB*

---

*You must understand this, my beloved:*
*let everyone be quick to listen,*
*slow to speak, slow to anger.*

*JAMES 1:19 NRSV*

You always grow to love the people you pray for.
That's because you develop God's heart of love for them.
Don't pass up the chance to experience that.

A good deed is never lost; he who sows courtesy
reaps friendship, and he who plants kindness gathers love.

*BASIL*

*Perfume and incense bring joy to the heart,*
*and the pleasantness of a friend*
*springs from their heartfelt advice.*

PROVERBS 27:9 NIV

Don't walk in front of me, I may not follow.
Don't walk behind me, I may not lead.
Walk beside me and just be my friend.

*ALBERT CAMUS*

Compassionate the mountains rise
Dim with the wistful dimness of old eyes
That, having looked on life time out of mind,
Know that the simple gift of being kind
Is greater than all wisdom of the wise.

*DUBOSE HEYWARD*

Life is but a brief moment between eternities.
There is no better time than now to assess the values
which are worthy of our existence on this earth.

*JAMES DOBSON*

We all stumble, every one of us.
That's why it's a comfort to go hand in hand.

*EMILY KIMBROUGH*

Friends help us feel secure. Our footing is surer
when we know that someone accepts us as we are,
someone has our best interests at heart, someone is always
glad to see us, someone plans to stick around.
There are few blessings like the blessing of a friend.

*EMILIE BARNES AND DONNA OTTO*

It is the purest sign that we love someone
if we choose to spend time idly in their presence
when we could be doing something more constructive.

*S. CASSIDY*

*May the Lord keep watch between you and me*
*when we are away from each other.*

GENESIS 31:49 NIV

*The Lord is gracious and merciful, slow to anger and abounding in steadfast love. The Lord is good to all, and His compassion is all over that He has made.*

PSALM 145:8-9 NRSV

A true friend is the gift of God, and He only
who made hearts can unite them.

*ROBERT SOUTH*

Open your hearts to the love God instills....
God loves you tenderly. What He gives you
is not to be kept under lock and key, but to be shared.

*MOTHER TERESA*

Eating lunch with a friend. Trying to do a decent day's work.
Hearing the rain patter against the window. There is
no event so commonplace but that God is present within it,
always hiddenly, always leaving you room to recognize Him.

*FREDERICK BUECHNER*

For all of us, whether we walk old paths or blaze new trails,
friends remain important.

*LOIS WYSE*

Keep thou thy dreams — the tissue of all wings
Is woven first of them; from dreams are made
The precious and imperishable things,
Whose loveliness lives on, and does not fade.

*VIRNA SHEARD*

If we would build on a sure foundation in friendship,
we must love our friends for their sakes rather than our own.

*CHARLOTTE BRONTË*

What is it about the confidence of others that makes us do things we could never do alone?

*TRACI DEPREE*

Few things heal wounded spirits better
than the balm of a supportive embrace.

CHARLES SWINDOLL

What brings joy to the heart is not so much
the friend's gifts as the friend's love.

*AILRED OF RIEVAULX*

---

*Let love be your greatest aim.*

*1 CORINTHIANS 14:1 TLB*

*See to it that you really do love each other warmly,*
*with all your hearts.*

1 PETER 1:22 TLB

Is life not full of opportunities for learning love? Every man and woman, every day, has a thousand of them....
And the one eternal lesson for us all is how better we can love.

*HENRY DRUMMOND*

We can never untangle all the woes in other people's lives.
We can't produce miracles overnight. But we can bring
a cup of cool water to a thirsty soul, or a scoop of laughter
to a lonely heart.

BARBARA JOHNSON

Normal day, let me be aware
of the treasure you are.
Let me learn from you, love you,
bless you before you depart.
Let me not pass you by in quest
of some rare and perfect tomorrow.

No love, no friendship can cross the path of our destiny

without leaving some mark on it forever.

FRANÇOIS MAURIAC

A fiery sunset, tiny pansies by the wayside, the sound of raindrops tapping on the roof—what an extraordinary delight to share simple wonders with a true friend! With wide eyes and full hearts, we come to cherish what others have missed.

A true friend is one who hears and understands
when you share your deepest feelings.... A true friend
prods you to personal growth, stretches you
to your full potential. And most amazing of all,
she celebrates your successes as if they were her own.

*RICHARD EXLEY*

As we grow in our capacities to see and enjoy the joys
that God has placed in our lives, life becomes a glorious
experience of discovering His endless wonders.

God in His ample love embraces our love with…
a sort of tenderness, and we must tread
the way to Him hand in hand.

*SHELDON VANAUKEN*

*Whatever is true, whatever is noble, whatever is right,
whatever is pure, whatever is lovely, whatever is admirable—
if anything is excellent or praiseworthy—think about such things.*

PHILIPPIANS 4:8 NIV

There are "friends" who pretend to be friends,
but there is a friend who sticks closer than a brother.

PROVERBS 18:24 TLB

Today a new sun rises for me; everything lives,
everything is animated, everything seems to speak to me
of my passion, everything invites me to cherish it.

*ANNE DE LENCLOS*

We were created to draw life and nourishment
from one another the way the roots of an oak tree draw life
from the soil. Community—living in vital connectedness
with others—is essential to human life.

*JOHN ORTBERG*

You entered my life in a casual way, and saw at a glance
what I needed. There were others who passed me
or met me each day, but never a one of them heeded.

*GRACE STRICKER DAWSON*

Friends are an indispensable part of a meaningful life.
They are the ones who share our burdens
and multiply our blessings.

*BEVERLY LAHAYE*

Loving and being loved is the greatest of human joys,
the ultimate human experience. We can exist without love,
but we are not living fully as human beings without it.

*EDWARD E. FORD*

Whenever I've needed someone to share my joy,
or someone to hold me when my world rips to pieces,
you're there. And I know you will be—tomorrow, always.

*MAYA V. PATEL*

The capacity of a woman's heart for meaningful relationships
is vast. There is no way your husband or your children
can ever provide the intimacy and relationship you need.
A woman must have woman friends.

*STASI ELDREDGE*

I want to help you to grow as beautiful
as God meant you to be
when He thought of you first.

*GEORGE MACDONALD*

*You gave me life and showed me kindness,*
*and in Your providence watched over my spirit.*

JOB 10:12 NIV

The loss of a friend is like that of a limb. Time may heal the anguish of the wound, but the loss cannot be repaired.

*ROBERT SOUTHY*

What made us friends in the long ago
When we first met?
Well, I think I know;
The best in me and the best in you
Hailed each other because they knew
That always and always since life began
Our being friends was part of God's plan.

GEORGE WEBSTER DOUGLAS

We may ask for greater faith so that we can heal others,
but God, who understands human need far better than we do,
gives us greater compassion so that we can weep with others.

*RICHARD J. FOSTER*

We must not cease from exploration and the end
of all our exploring will be to arrive where we began
and to know the place for the first time.

*T.S. ELIOT*

*I thank my God every time I remember you.*
*In all my prayers for all of you, I always pray with joy.*

PHILIPPIANS 1:3-4 NIV

Are you aware that the Father takes delight in you
and that He thinks about you all the time?

*JACK FROST*

Kind words are jewels that live in the heart and soul
and remain as blessed memories
years after they have been spoken.

*MARVEA JOHNSON*

On those days when my socks don't match up, I...find ways
to be happy. The easiest way for me to do this is to call up
a friend and share a joke. When I see or hear one I really like,
I keep it by the phone so I can remember to tell it to the friends
who call. Just yesterday I was delighted to call my friends
and share a funny bumper sticker I'd seen that morning....
"Driver Carries No Cash—(He's Married)."

*BARBARA JOHNSON*

Our Father, we thank You for trees! We thank You
for the trees of our childhood in whose shade we played
and read and dreamed; for the trees of our schooldays,
the trees along the paths where friendship walked.

MARGUERITE HARMON

*In everything you do, put God first, and He will direct you and crown your efforts with success.*

PROVERBS 3:6 TLB

May your footsteps set you upon a lifetime journey of love.
May you wake each day with His blessings
and sleep each night in His keeping.
And may you always walk in His tender care.

There is no place to go, and so we travel!
You and I, and what for, just to imagine
that we could go somewhere else.

EDWARD DAHLBERG

*I will send down showers in season;*
*there will be showers of blessing.*
*The trees will yield their fruit*
*and the ground will yield its crops;*
*the people will be secure in their land.*

EZEKIEL 34:26-27 NIV

Such is friendship, that through it we love places and seasons; for as bright bodies emit rays to a distance, and flowers drop their sweet leaves on the ground around them, so friends impart favor even to the places where they dwell.

JOHN CHRYSOSTOM

God loves us too much to leave us muddling about
in our sin. No matter what our problem—lying, cheating,
marital unfaithfulness, yelling at the kids, fudging on
the income tax, bitterness, anger, gossip, etc., etc.—
God is tenacious in His commitment to developing us
into people of integrity who love Him, reflect Him
to others, and delight in doing His will.

MARILYN MERBERG

Take time to notice all the usually unnoticed,
simple things in life. Delight in the never-ending hope
that's available every day!

We love our friends by pursuing them—calls, little presents, cards, invitations to play, to go for a walk, to go to a movie. We offer our hearts.

*STASI ELDRIDGE*

When our relationships are born in the heart of God,
they bring out the best in us, for they are nurtured by love.

*DON LESSIN*

If you are skilled in a particular arena in which someone
you love is having trouble, send an encouraging e-mail.
God will honor your kindness, and your friend will feel better.

---

*Lord, how can I encourage someone today?*
*Show me, then help me to do it. Amen.*

LUCI SWINDOLL

*For if you give, you will get! Your gift will return to you in full and overflowing measure, pressed down, shaken together to make room for more, and running over. Whatever measure you use to give—large or small—will be used to measure what is given back to you.*

LUKE 6:38 TLB

*We're just God's servants, each of us with certain special abilities...*
*But it was God...who made the garden grow in your hearts.*

1 CORINTHIANS 3:5-7 TLB

There is no more significant involvement in another's life
than prevailing, consistent prayer. It is more helpful
than a gift of money, more encouraging than a strong sermon,
more effective than a compliment, more reassuring
than a physical embrace.

*CHARLES SWINDOLL*

When seeds of kindness are sown prayerfully
in the garden plot of our lives, we may be sure
that there will be a bountiful harvest of blessings
for both us and others.

*W. PHILLIP KELLER*

There is no friend like the old friend
who has shared our morning days,
No greeting like his praise;
Fame is the scentless sunflower,
with gaudy crown of gold;
But friendship is the breathing rose,
with sweets in every fold.

*OLIVER WENDELL HOLMES*

I breathed a song into the air; It fell to earth,
I know not where…and the song, from beginning to end,
I found again in the heart of a friend.

*LONGFELLOW*

We need time to dream, time to remember,
and time to reach the infinite. Time to be.

*GLADYS TABER*

In God's wisdom, He frequently chooses
to meet our needs by showing His love toward us
through the hands and hearts of others.

*JACK HAYFORD*

Rest is not idleness, and to lie sometimes on the grass
under trees on a summer's day, listening to the murmur
of the water, or watching the clouds float across the sky,
is by no means a waste of time.

*SIR JOHN LUBBOCK*

Live for something…. Write your name in kindness,
love, and mercy on the hearts of thousands
you come in contact with…. You will never be forgotten.

*THOMAS CHALMERS*

*So I pray for you...that God who gives you hope will keep you happy and full of peace as you believe in Him.*

ROMANS 15:13 TLB

*Keep on sowing your seed, for you never know
which will grow—perhaps it all will.*

ECCLESIASTES 11:6 TLB

I have never known anyone who succeeded at relationships—
who cultivated great friendships, who was devoted
to his or her family, who mastered the art of giving
and receiving love—yet had a bad life.

JOHN ORTBERG

It is an awesome, challenging thought:
The Lord comes to us in our friends.
What we do and are to them is an expression
of what we are to Him.

*LLOYD JOHN OGILVIE*

Every act of kindness
Moves to a larger one
Till friendships bloom to show
What little deeds have done.

*JUNE MASTERS BACHER*

Knowing what to say is not always necessary;
just the presence of a caring friend
can make a world of difference.

*SHERI CURRY*

Love means to love that which is unlovable, or it is no virtue at all; forgiving means to pardon that which is unpardonable, or it is no virtue at all—and to hope means hoping when things are hopeless, or it is no virtue at all.

*G.K. CHESTERTON*

I know that God is at work in the regularness of my days.

May I recognize His hand when I see it.

*GLORIA GAITHER*

The true way and the sure way to friendship
is through humility—being open to each other,
accepting each other just as we are, knowing each other.

*MOTHER TERESA*

There are moments when our hearts nearly burst within us for the sheer joy of being alive. The first sight of our newborn babies, the warmth of love in another's eyes, the fresh scent of rain on a hot summer's eve—moments like these renew in us a heartfelt appreciation for life.

*GWEN ELLIS*

Every single act of love bears the imprint of God.

*Most important of all, continue to show deep love for each other,*
*for love makes up for many of your faults.*

1 PETER 4:8 TLB

Loneliness isn't a bad thing, except when
you don't have anyone to share it with.

BARBARA JOHNSON

*Share each other's troubles and problems,
and so obey our Lord's command.*

GALATIANS 6:2 TLB

At every crossroad, follow your dream.
It is courageous to let your heart lead the way.

*THOMAS LELAND*

Communication means a sharing together of what you really are. With the stethoscope of love you listen until you hear the heartbeat of the other.

*BARTLETT AND MARGARET HESS*

I still find each day too short for all the thoughts
I want to think, all the walks I want to take, all the books
I want to read, and all the friends I want to see.
The longer I live, the more my mind dwells upon
the beauty and the wonder of the world.

*JOHN BURROUGHS*

We all mold one another's dreams. We all hold each other's fragile hopes in our hands. We all touch others' hearts.

A true friend is one who is concerned about what
we are becoming, who sees beyond the present relationship,
and who cares deeply about us as a whole person.

*GLORIA GAITHER*

For memory has painted this perfect day with colors
that never fade. And we find at the end of a perfect day,
the soul of a friend we've made.

CARRIE JACOBS BOND

I have a garden of my own,
Shining with flowers of every hue;
I loved it dearly while alone,
But I shall love it more with you.

*THOMAS MOORE*

Old friends are the great blessing of one's latter years.
Half a word conveys one's meaning. They have a memory
for the same events, and have the same mode of thinking.

HORACE WALPOLE

*Be kind to one another, tenderhearted, forgiving one another,*
*as God in Christ has forgiven you.*

EPHESIANS 4:32 NRSV

*From a wise mind comes careful and persuasive speech.*
*Kind words are like honey—enjoyable and healthful.*

PROVERBS 16:23-24 TLB

A true friend sticks by us in our joys and sorrows.
In good times and bad, we need friends who will pray for us,
listen to us, and lend a comforting hand
and understanding ear when needed.

*BEVERLY LAHAYE*

The fountain of beauty is the heart,
and every generous thought
illustrates the walls of your chamber.

*FRANCIS QUARLES*

We have a price to pay for depth
in sharing in another's life.
And the one payment that will yield
the greatest interest is time together.

*JACK MAYHALL*

Only the heart knows how to find what is precious.

FYODOR DOSTOYEVSKY

*Above all else, guard your heart,*
*for everything you do flows from it.*

PROVERBS 4:23 NIV

All that we have and are is one of the unique and never-to-be
repeated ways God has chosen to express Himself in space
and time. Each of us, made in His image and likeness,
is yet another promise He has made to the universe
that He will continue to love it and care for it.

*BRENNAN MANNING*

Whatever leisure time we are able to invest
in relationships is time well spent.

CHARLES SWINDOLL

---

*Teach us to number our days and recognize how few they are;*
*help us to spend them as we should.*

PSALM 90:12 TLB

The God who created, names, and numbers the stars
in the heavens also numbers the hairs on my head....
He pays attention to very big things and to very small ones.
What matters to me matters to Him, and that changes my life.

*ELISABETH ELLIOT*

We are truly loving when we help ourselves and others
to be all we are meant to be. A loving life is a life
where there is a balance between fulfilling our own needs
and caring enough about others to help them fulfill theirs.

*ALEXANDRA STODDARD*

*I will very gladly spend for you everything I have
and expend myself as well.*

2 CORINTHIANS 12:15 NIV

*You are joined together with peace through the Spirit,
so make every effort to continue together in this way.*

EPHESIANS 4:3 NCV

A knowledge that another has felt as we have felt,
and seen things not much otherwise than we have seen them,
will continue to the end to be one of life's choicest blessings.

ROBERT LOUIS STEVENSON

Hand Grasps at hand, eye lights eye in good friendship,
And great hearts expand
And grow one in the sense of this world's life.

*ROBERT BROWNING*

There can be no friendship when there is no freedom.
Friendship loves the free air, and will not be fenced up
in straight and narrow enclosures.

WILLIAM PENN

We are very rich if we know just a few people
in a way in which we know no others.

CATHERINE BRAMWELL-BOOTH

It is only with the heart that one can see rightly.
What is essential is invisible to the eye.

*ANTOINE DE SAINT-EXPUPÉRY*

Beautiful and rich is an old friendship.
Grateful to the touch as ancient ivory,
Smooth as aged wine, or sheen of tapestry
Where light has lingered, intimate and long.

*EUNICE TIETJENS*

True friendships are lasting because true love is eternal.
A friendship in which heart speaks to heart is a gift
from God, and no gift that comes from God
is temporary or occasional.

*HENRI J.M. NOUWEN*

The human contribution is the essential ingredient.
It is only in the giving of oneself to oneself that we truly live.

*ETHEL PERCY ANDRUS*

*How precious it is, Lord, to realize that You are thinking about me*
*constantly! I can't even count how many times a day*
*Your thoughts turn toward me. And when I waken*
*in the morning, You are still thinking of me!*

PSALM 139:17-18 TLB